# The Magic Bicycle Ride

Sally Sheringham



Illustrated by Robin Lawrie

Hamlyn

London · New York · Sydney · Toronto

# Contents

# Topsy-turvy land

It was a sunny spring afternoon.

Sue, Paul, and William – their black and white dog – lay on the lawn with nothing to do. They felt hot, bad-tempered and, most of all, *bored*.

'I wish something exciting would happen,' sighed Sue.

'So do I,' said Paul, idly watching William wandering over to the bushes. 'If I look at my comic once more I think I'll scream.'

'If I look at *you* once more I think I'll scream,' laughed Sue, then ducked as Paul threw a handful of grass at her.

Suddenly, William started barking. 'Let's go and see what he's found,' said Sue.

'Okay,' said Paul. 'Anything's better than having to lie here talking to you.'

They chased each other across the lawn. In the distance they heard their father shouting that it was tea-time.

'Coming in a minute,' yelled Sue as they crashed through the bushes.

William had stopped barking now and, although they searched everywhere, they couldn't find him. What they did find, though, was an old, rusty, black and white, two-seater bicycle.

'Where on earth has this old thing come from?' asked Sue. 'And where's William? You know, if I believed in magic, I'd have

said that he'd turned into this bicycle.'

'Trust *you* to believe in magic,' said Paul. 'Shall we have a ride on it?'

They climbed on, Sue on the front and Paul on the back. It was the perfect size, and they had great fun weaving in and out of the bushes. They had quite forgotten to look for William – or that it was tea-time.

'Wouldn't it be great,' said Sue suddenly, 'if it could fly.'

'Don't be daft,' said Paul. 'Things like that only happen in books.' And then his mouth dropped open. For, after a bump and a thump, the bicycle left the ground. They *were* flying! They watched their house and garden, then their street, then the town, get smaller and smaller as they flew up into the blue sky.

'Are we dreaming, or is this really happening?' shouted Paul. (He had to shout because of the wind.)

'Two people don't have the same dream, so it must be happening,' said Sue. 'Hold on tight.'

Feeling a bit sick, she looked down. The town was now just a tiny little dot. And then she

couldn't see it at all because clouds, looking like giant pieces of white candy-floss, had got in the way. 'Wouldn't it be exciting if we landed in some strange land, where everything's different?' she said.

The bicycle swung to the left and, within a few minutes, that's exactly what happened. They had

landed – bump! – in a field that was totally different to any field they'd ever seen before. For the grass was pink, the trees were growing upside-down, the cows were walking on their hind legs and all the birds were flying backwards!

Sue and Paul got off the bicycle, leant it against a gate shaped like a snail's shell, and looked round.

'What a very odd place,' said Sue. 'I wonder where we are.'

And then they saw an even odder sight – a broomstick chasing a mouse. Above them, a big black cat flew through the air with a witch riding on its back!

'I hope she's a friendly witch,' whispered Paul as she landed right beside them.

'Welcome to Topsy-turvy land,' she boomed, sliding off the big black cat's back and landing – bonk! – on her nose. 'And what can I do for you?' she asked, brushing pink grass off her pointed blue hat. 'I specialize in love spells and making young men taller. Hmmm, you could do with being taller,' she said, looking Paul up and down.

Sue giggled and Paul, whose cheeks had turned pink, said quickly, 'Actually, we are looking for our dog, William.'

'Dog . . . dog,' said the witch, scratching her thin nose. 'I've never done a dog spell, but there's always a first time. Follow me!'

And so they all flew to her cottage, which was bright green – it even had bright green smoke

coming from the chimney. Inside, it was full of bubbling cauldrons and spellbooks covered in cobwebs.

'Now, let's see,' said the witch, putting on a pair of bright green spectacles, blowing a cloud of dust off her largest spell book and reading it upside-down. 'Ah yes,' she said and put some cough mixture, a dead mouse and a pair of purple socks into a bubbling cauldron. Then, giving it a quick stir with a feather duster, she did a little dance and out of the cauldron popped . . . a hot dog!

Sue and Paul's faces fell.

'Is that William?' asked the witch doubtfully.

The children shook their heads and so, with a wave of the feather duster, the hot dog was gone.

Then the witch cleared her throat. 'Between you and me,' she said, rather embarrassed, 'I'm not sure what a dog looks like.'

So Sue and Paul tried to describe William.

'He has four legs and pointed ears.'

'And a long bendy tail.'

'He's a little bit plump.'

'And has a rather pointed nose.'

'And is the nicest dog in the world.'

'And . . .'

'That's enough, thank you,' said the witch excitedly. 'I can picture him very clearly.'

This time she put into the bubbling cauldron a chicken's feather, a gold button, two green beetles, an ice-cream cone and a lettuce leaf, and slowly uttered a magic rhyme in a deep voice. Suddenly, the cauldron started hissing green smoke and then out popped the strangest animal the children had ever seen. He had a round body and was covered in bright green fur. He looked as much like William as a rabbit looks like a tiger.

'Is that William?' asked the witch hopefully.

Sue nudged Paul. 'Er – yes it is,' he said. 'Thank you very much.'

'No trouble,' said the witch. 'Happy to oblige.'

'Well, we must be going,' said Paul. 'Come along, William.'

So William, who wasn't really William of course, followed them outside to the bicycle. He fitted perfectly in the basket on the front. After waving goodbye to the

witch, the bicycle took off and they were soon flying up in the clouds again.

Paul and Sue were just talking about what a strange day it was turning out to be, when suddenly the green animal spoke!

'Hmph,' it said. 'William indeed. What a silly name. My name's Sir Parsnip Wilberforce Periwinkle Alarm-clock Smythe, and don't you forget it. You can call me Prunes for short if you like,' he added kindly.

'How do you do, Prunes,' said Paul, trying not to laugh. 'I'm Paul and that's my sister Sue.'

'Hello,' said Prunes. 'May I enquire where we're going?'

'Your guess is as good as ours,' said Paul.

'Only the bicycle knows,' said Sue.

'Crumbs,' said Prunes. 'Well, wherever it is, I hope we get there soon. I'm getting squashed.'

The bicycle gave a little lurch, and continued to race on through the sky.

# The royal palace

They had been flying for what seemed like several hours, when suddenly they came across a huge palace.

'Crumbs,' said Prunes as they narrowly missed a turret. And then they were landing, right in the middle of the lawn.

‘Crumbs,’ said Prunes again as the courtiers, wearing long curly wigs and beautiful clothes, gathered round them and said things like ‘How charming’ and ‘What sweet children’.

And then a trumpeter in white breeches played a short fanfare, and everyone began to bow or curtsy. The king and queen had arrived.

‘Hadn’t we better bow and curtsy, too?’ Paul whispered. So they got off the bicycle and, in the

confusion, as Sue and Paul bowed, Prunes curtsied! Everyone roared with laughter.

'I see that you're not used to meeting kings and queens,' laughed the red-faced king, patting them on the head. 'Don't

worry, it won't take long to learn all there is to know.'

Paul, who didn't like being patted on the head, said, 'I don't think we'll be staying all that long, your – er – majesties.'

'No. We're just on a flying visit,' added Prunes, and everyone laughed again.

'Oh, come now,' said the king. 'We so rarely have visitors, let alone *children* visitors. *Do* stay. You'll be treated like kings.'

'Like a king and a queen, don't you mean, dear,' said the queen.

'Quite so,' said the king. 'You see, my dears, we don't have any children of our own, so if you stay here, you may become the king and queen yourselves, one day!'

The children looked at each other doubtfully. They had often played kings and queens at home, using the clothes out of the dressing-up box, but that was only pretend. It was a very different matter being a *real* king or queen.

'But . . .' began Paul.

'No buts,' said the queen. 'Now, first we must take you into the palace and get you out of those frightful clothes.'

So, while the bicycle was housed in the royal stables, the children

and Prunes followed the queen into the palace. What a contrast it was to the witch's dusty, musty old place! There were gold statues and marble floors and lights that sparkled like stars. The red stair carpet was so thick they felt as if they were walking through long grass. The stair rail was made of solid gold.

'I'd love to slide down that,' whispered Prunes.

The queen swept down long corridors and it was difficult not to

tread on her long satin gown. Once Prunes did step on it. The look the queen gave him wasn't a friendly one.

She led them into a huge bedroom. A row of maids in long white aprons and frilly white caps all curtsied when they entered.

'Now,' said the queen to the maids, 'I want these children – and this, er, creature – bathed and

dressed in the finest clothes in the palace. Anything you want, my dears,' she said, turning to the children, 'just ask.'

'I'd like a hamburger and chips and a strawberry milk shake, please,' said Prunes. Fortunately for Prunes, the queen was rather deaf.

One of the maids stepped forward. 'If you would like to get

undressed, sirs and madam, your bath is ready for you.'

Sirs and madam! They'd never been called that before. How important it made them feel.

'I'm not going to undress in front of all those maids,' whispered Paul, turning red.

'They're far too polite to look,' answered Sue. And she was right.

What fun it was having a bath in a tub as big as a paddling pool. 'This is the life,' Prunes said as one maid cut his toe-nails and another washed his back.

When they got out they found big, clean white towels waiting for them, and their clothes laid out on the bed – and what clothes! Paul

put on pale green silk trousers that ended at the knee, white stockings and shoes with silver buckles, a shirt with lace down the front and a hat with a floppy brim and a large purple feather.

'I look soppy,' he said when he looked at himself in the mirror.

'We think you look very nice – a real young gentleman,' said the maids.

Paul turned red. But he didn't moan about his clothes again.

Sue, meanwhile, had put on three long petticoats, a long blue dress with pearl buttons, long white lace gloves and silver high-heel shoes. The maids curled up her long hair. How grown-up she looked. This was much better than anything out of the dressing-up box.

The maids tied a big floppy velvet bow tie round Prunes' neck. 'Crumbs,' he said as he looked in the mirror.

Then the head maid led them to the court room. There sat the king and queen on their thrones. 'Ah, my dears. That's more like it,' said the queen, taking no notice of Prunes. 'You look just like a prince and princess. And now we will

begin to teach you how to *behave* like a prince and princess.'

'Don't mind me,' muttered Prunes.

And so their training began. They were taught how to bow and curtsy properly, how to address the courtiers, and the servants, and always to say please and thank you. They were taught the correct way to eat the royal foods,

to sit up straight, never to talk with their mouths full and never to laugh unless the king and queen laughed first. They were taught to ride ponies and play games. Meanwhile, Prunes, to his fury, was being taught how to be a royal pet. 'I'm not a pet, I'm Prunes,' he grumbled.

At first the children enjoyed being the centre of attraction and being given anything they asked for. But one day, when they were playing with their royal toys in the playroom, Paul said, 'I'm getting really fed up with all this. I'm not sure I want to be a king.'

'I'm not sure I want to be a queen, either,' said Sue. 'It's such hard work always being on your best behaviour.'

'Quite agree,' said Prunes, stuffing a whole sausage roll into his mouth in one go. 'I'd love to be really rude to everyone.'

'Shall we leave them?' said Paul.

'I thought you'd never ask,' said Prunes. 'But before we go, I'm going to do some really naughty

things to pay them back for treating me like a pet.'

That night there was a grand supper, when Sue and Paul had to make polite conversation to a boring duke and duchess. But afterwards, when everyone had gone to

bed, they changed back into their comfortable old clothes. Then they wrote a note to the king and queen saying they were sorry but they weren't cut out to be a king and queen. Next, while they crept out to fetch the bicycle, Prunes set to work. First he put green colouring on the queen's false-teeth, then hid the king's wig in a cupboard. He drew moustaches and beards on the royal

family portraits and slid down that lovely gold stair rail. He was just about to creep into the kitchen and swop the salt with the sugar and the cheese with the soap, when he heard a shout. He dashed out to where the children were waiting. They leapt on to the bicycle and were just about to take off when out ran the queen with green teeth and the king with a shiny bald head. 'Come back you wicked children,' they roared.

'Cheerio – and good riddance,' shouted Prunes cheekily as the bicycle took off into the night. 'I feel like a new animal now I can be rude again,' he said, settling into the basket. 'Wasn't the queen horrible? She reminded me of a fat toad.'

The children laughed. 'It's good to have you back to your usual rude self,' said Paul.

Then, as they travelled through the black, starless sky, Prunes said, 'Between you and me, I'm looking for somewhere to settle

down – you know, make myself a home. I've had enough of travelling.'

'Maybe the next place where we land will be suitable,' said Sue. 'Though goodness knows what sort of place it'll be.'

'Knowing my luck it'll be horrible,' said Prunes.

As it turned out, he wasn't far off the truth.

# The land of the Horribles

It was just getting light when the children, Prunes and the bicycle landed in the middle of a dark, unfriendly-looking wood. A pair of yellow eyes stared at them and they could hear scary rustling

sounds from the bushes. Sue and Paul shivered, and even Prunes looked slightly nervous.

'Hello. Anyone at home?' he shouted bravely, though his voice had a tremble to it.

Suddenly, something black fluttered in their faces. Sue screamed.

'Friend or foe?' asked Prunes in his sternest voice.

The thing fluttered a bit more before hanging, upside-down, on a branch of a twisted oak tree. It was a large black bat.

None of them liked bats very much, and they certainly didn't like this one. Nor did they like all the eyes that were staring at them from holes in trees, through bushes and from behind plants. They were just about to get back on the bicycle and ask it to fly away from this horrible place, when the bat said, very politely, 'So frightfully sorry if I scared you.'

'Crumbs,' whispered Prunes. 'He's a gentleman. Honestly. First a snooty king and queen and now a snooty bat. Can't get away from them.'

'Could you tell us where we are, please?' said Sue to the bat.

'The land of the Horribles,' said

the bat, giving an upside-down bow.

The children looked alarmed.

'Oh, don't worry,' said the bat. 'We aren't really horrible. We just look horrible. Let me explain. All the animals who live here are considered "horrible" by everyone else. We all got so fed-up with people hating us because we

looked horrible that we decided to live together here. And very happy we are, too. Care to look round?'

Sue and Paul weren't very keen on meeting lots of horrible animals. But before they had a chance to say anything, Prunes said, 'Oh, yes please.'

And so began the strangest visit the children had ever been on, in this gloomy land where creepy-crawlies winked from the roots of trees and where bugs and slugs giggled from under their stones.

First of all, the bat, whose name was Harold, introduced them to

four big rats who were having an early-morning game of tennis.

'Trying to keep fit, you know,' said one of them, slapping his round tummy and grinning. Seeing all those sharp yellow teeth made Susan shiver. She *hated* rats. And yet she had to admit, these ones were very friendly, offering her orange juice and inviting her back to their homes for breakfast. 'You see, we aren't so horrible, after all,' they said, before returning to their game of tennis.

'And now meet a snake,' said Harold. This time it was Paul's turn to shiver. He was terrified of snakes. And when one slithered round his neck he couldn't help screaming.

'No need to be frightened. It's only my way of saying hello,' said the snake, offering his tail to be shaken. 'Delighted to meet you.'

Paul began to relax slightly and, when the snake turned out to be a keen football fan, he actually began to *like* him. They spent a

long time happily discussing the game.

Meanwhile, Prunes suddenly began to pull horrible faces. First he pulled his lips back into a snarl, then he wrinkled his face up till it looked like a crumpled paper bag.

'Why are you pulling those horrible faces?' asked Sue.

'I like it here,' said Prunes, 'because I don't feel out of place. People don't stare at me because I look funny, because they all look funny, too. I'm trying to make myself look as horrible as possible so that they'll let me live here,' he said, crossing his eyes and sticking out his tongue.

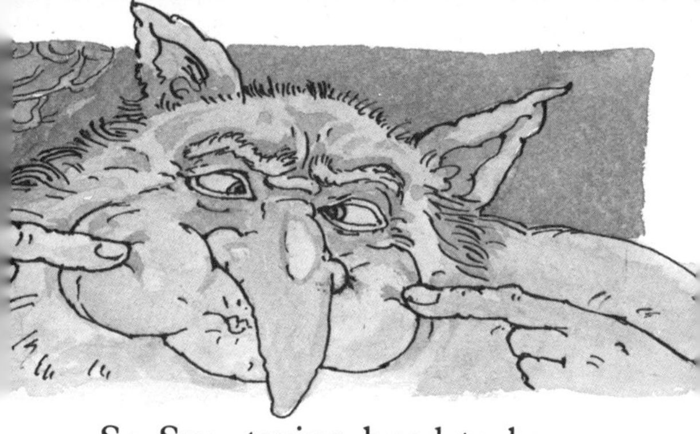

So Sue, trying hard to keep a straight face, had a word with Harold. He looked at Prunes, who was puffing out his cheeks.

'Hmmm, I agree, he is pretty horrible,' said Harold. 'I'll have to call a meeting so that everyone can decide whether he's horrible enough to live here.' And he let out a shrill scream.

Soon, Sue, Paul and Prunes

were surrounded by the most horrible animals they'd ever seen – as well as the rats and snakes, there were spiders, slugs, vultures, crocodiles, insects and big fat creepy-crawlies.

'Ladies and gentlemen,' shouted Harold when all the animals had assembled. 'Today we have a very important decision to make. May I present to you Prunes . . .' and Prunes stepped forward, a wicked snarl on his face, 'who wants to make the land of the Horribles his home. We have to decide whether he's horrible enough. Your opinions, please.'

Everyone stared at Prunes, who

stared back through squinting eyes. Paul and Sue found it hard not to laugh.

‘He’s got horrible legs,’ growled Crocodile.

‘And a horrible face,’ squawked Vulture.

‘I bet he smells horrible,’ said Skunk.

‘He’s certainly a horrible colour,’ buzzed Blue Bottle.

‘I think,’ squeaked Slug, ‘that

he's altogether too horrible for words.'

'Do we all agree on that?' asked Harold.

'Yes,' shouted all the Horribles.

'In that case,' said Harold, turning to Prunes, 'welcome to your new home.'

Everyone cheered and crowded

round Prunes, who had forgotten to look horrible and was now grinning broadly. Champagne corks started popping, and a band of wasps started playing a merry tune. Soon everyone was dancing, and a great time was had by all.

After Paul and Sue had danced with almost every animal, includ-

ing the insects, Paul said they'd better be going.

'Not going so soon, old fruits, are you?' asked Harold. 'Why, the party's only just beginning.'

'I'm afraid we've got to find our dog,' said Sue. 'You haven't seen him, have you? His name's William.'

Harold shook his head. 'Dogs aren't nearly horrible enough to come here. Tell you what, why don't you try the planet of the dogs? It's not far away. Turn right, then left, then it's straight ahead. Don't tell them you've come from here, though. They

hate us.'

All the Horribles came to see them off. Due to one too many glasses of champagne, Prunes had gone slightly cross-eyed without even trying. He shook them both by the hand. 'I'm going to miss you,' he said.

'We're going to miss you, too,' said Sue, kissing his green cheek. 'I hope you'll be very happy here.' Then she quickly turned and got on the bicycle so that he wouldn't notice the tear that trickled down her cheek.

'Come back soon,' shouted the Horribles as the bicycle took off. The children waved until they were out of sight.

'Well,' said Paul. 'I never thought I'd live to see the day when I'd make friends with a snake!'

'Yes, they were all nice,' said Sue. 'But Prunes was the nicest of all. I am going to miss him.'

'So am I,' said Paul.

After they had been flying for a while, Paul said, 'I hope the bicycle knows the way to the planet of the dogs.' Just at that moment, it swung to the right, then to the left.

'Of course it does,' said Sue. 'Remember, this is no ordinary bicycle.'

Never had truer words been said.

# The planet of the dogs

'Look,' shouted Paul suddenly, 'that must be the planet of the dogs.'

And, ahead of them, in the middle of the sky, was what looked like a giant bone.

The bone got bigger and bigger as they got closer. Soon they could see houses shaped like dog kennels and then they were landing, right in the middle of the town square.

Immediately they were surrounded by dogs of all shapes and sizes. And, the funny thing about them was, they all stood on their hind legs and wore clothes, like humans.

'I say, I haven't seen a bicycle for years,' said a Labrador wearing a checked cap and smoking a pipe. 'We all use cars here, you know.'

'Ah, but cars can't fly like our bicycle can,' said Paul.

'No,' said the Labrador's wife, who had a copy of *The Sporting Dog* under her arm. 'But helicopters can.'

And, just at that very moment, a red helicopter shaped like a dog landed in the middle of the town square.

Out climbed a plump bulldog wearing a pinstripe suit, a bowler hat and a gold chain round his neck. His wife wore a hat covered in cherries with a dress to match. She had difficulty in walking over

the cobblestones in her high-heel shoes.

'They're even uglier than our mayor and mayoress at home,' whispered Paul.

'Shhh,' giggled Sue. 'They're coming over.'

'Welcome to the planet of the dogs,' boomed the mayor, offering his plump sweaty paw for the children to shake.

'How do you do, er . . .'

'Your worships, if you please,' said the mayor.

'Your worships,' mumbled Paul and Sue.

'May I ask where you've come from?' asked the mayor.

'Earth,' said Sue, remembering what Harold had said.

'Ah – Earth. That's all right then. For a minute I thought you might have come from the land of

the Horribles. Now, allow me and my good wife to show you around our fine town. But first, please put that bicycle out of sight. It's such an awful spectacle.'

So the children unwillingly wheeled the bicycle behind a fountain and then followed the mayor and mayoress round the town.

All the houses were shaped like kennels. One was called Poodle's Parlour. In the garden, a white poodle in an apron was picking dog roses. There was a hairdresser's called Fifi's Famous Furdressing Salon, where dogs sat in a row with rollers in their fur. They passed a school; a games lesson was going on. All the puppies, who wore shorts, were chasing a clockwork rabbit across the playground.

'Bet you don't do anything like that in your school, what!' laughed the mayor.

They passed a cinema showing two films called *Gone with the Hound* and *The Sound of Barking*.

'We show all the latest films here,' said the mayor proudly.

And all the time, Paul and Sue were looking out for William. They looked in the butcher's, where a corgi in an apron chopped meat; they looked in the toyshop, where a basset hound was selling a plastic rat to a puppy; they looked in a jeweller's, where a red setter was buying a gold collar for his wife.

'Somehow I can't imagine William living here. I don't think he'd fit in,' whispered Sue.

'I don't think *I* fit in, either,' said Paul.

'Anything wrong?' asked the mayor.

'Er, we're looking for our dog, William,' said Sue. 'I suppose you haven't come across him?'

The mayor wrinkled his brow even more than it was wrinkled already. 'I don't recall seeing any strangers recently. Tell you what, we'll go and ask at the town hall. They keep a record of all newcomers.'

So they went into the town hall, which was the shape of a giant dog biscuit. They walked over to a spaniel who, on seeing the mayor, dropped all his papers. When he bent down to pick them up, his spectacles slid off the end of his nose.

'Ah, Mr Spillington-Spaniel,' said the mayor. 'Will you look through the files and see whether a William er . . . What's his surname?'

'He hasn't got one,' said Sue.

The mayor looked surprised. 'Well, what breed is he then?'

'Er, he's a mongrel,' said Paul.

The mayor's mouth dropped open, and the mayoress looked as though she were about to faint. Mr Spillington-Spaniel dropped his papers again. 'Did you say mongrel?' he said, his glasses slipping off his nose.

'Yes,' said Paul. 'What's wrong?'

'What's wrong? Everything's wrong,' boomed the mayor. 'All the dogs on this planet are pedigree dogs. We would never allow a mongrel to live here.'

'But he's a lovely dog,' said Sue.

'I dare say,' said the mayor. 'But still, I must ask you both to leave immediately. We don't have anything to do with people who like mongrels.'

Paul and Sue were now very angry. 'He's a far nicer dog than any of the ones who live here,' she said.

'Yes,' said Paul. 'He's worth a hundred of any of you lot.'

The mayor looked as though he were about to burst out of his suit he was so angry, while the mayoress actually did faint. The children ran like the wind out of the town hall, down the cobbled streets to the bicycle.

Already, word had got about.

Dogs were whispering and giggling and pointing, and a bull terrier actually shouted, 'Mongrels! Whatever next.'

The children leapt on to the bicycle, which was shaking with rage. Instead of taking off straight away, it charged down the street, causing the dogs to jump out of its way. In a real fury now, it went straight for the mayor and mayor-

ess. It ran over the mayor's shoe and then knocked off the mayoress's silly hat with its handlebars, as it flew off into the sky.

The children cheered. 'Well done, bicycle,' said Paul. 'What horrible, horrible dogs.'

'I wish Prunes had been there – he would have really told them what he thought of them,' said Sue. 'You know, I'm almost certain now that the bicycle is William. Why would he have got so cross otherwise?'

'You've got a point there,' admitted Paul. 'Well, William, where are you taking us to this time?'

But the bicycle – or was it William? – just flew up and up into the bright blue sky.

# The land of the purple men

This was definitely the strangest place Paul and Sue had been to so far. No trees or flowers grew, and no birds sang. Everything was purple – the ground, the dome-shaped buildings, even the cars, which were now zooming towards them. But they didn't look like ordinary cars – they were like tiny high-speed electric trains and made a quiet swishing noise.

'We must be somewhere in the future,' said Paul excitedly.

Out of these funny purple cars

jumped even funnier little purple men. They were the size of the children, even though they were fully grown. They had short, straight, purple hair parted in the middle, round purple faces and wore purple tracksuits and purple running shoes. But the strangest

thing about them was that they all had three eyes – two in the normal place and one in the middle of their foreheads. Suddenly, all these third eyes started beaming a purple ray of light at the children. It didn't hurt but it was very bright, and they had to close their eyes.

'What are you doing?' cried Sue.

'Just carrying out orders,' squeaked one of the purple men. 'We check all visitors to see whether they have weapons. Now that we've found out you haven't, our master would like to meet you.'

So the children and the bicycle followed the purple men into the

biggest of the purple domes. There, sitting in front of hundreds of television screens and thousands of dials and buttons, sat the master.

'Welcome to the planet Purple Three. Where do you come from?' asked the master. He looked just like all the other purple men except that his third eye wasn't purple but lilac-coloured. The children felt rather frightened.

'Earth,' said Sue.

'Ah, Earth. That's way behind the times – ten thousand years, as

can be seen from that old-fashioned flying machine of yours. But tell me – it has no wings or power – how does it fly?'

'We're not really sure,' said Paul.

The master frowned, which caused his middle eye to fold in two. 'But you *must* know. If you've invented a machine, then you must know how it works.'

'But we don't,' said Sue. 'We think it might be magic.'

'*Magic*?' exclaimed the master. 'But surely no one believes in magic these days, not even on Earth?'

The children couldn't think of anything to say.

'I would like some of my scientists to examine this unusual machine,' said the master.

Sue and Paul looked at the bicycle. It shook its front wheel.

'I'm afraid we can't allow that. It wouldn't like it at all,' said Sue, holding tightly on to the handlebars.

The master frowned again. How odd it made his middle eye look. 'As you wish,' he said. 'And now I would like you to look round Purple Three's museum.'

'Let's try and escape,' whispered Sue. But, before they could do anything, two purple men had sprung from nowhere and held on to their arms firmly.

'Follow me,' said the master.

And so they followed him out into this silent purple world, where cars made no more sound than a whisper and where there were no shops or children.

The master led them into a dome that was full of paintings of purple squiggles and blobs, unusually-shaped purple statues, a dome-shaped purple computer and lots of other modern machines that the children found a bit boring.

'And now I'd like to show you our only living exhibit,' said the master proudly, and he took them over to a purple cage. The children couldn't believe their eyes. For there, sitting behind the purple bars, looking very cross, was none

other than Prunes!

Sue was so amazed that she gasped. The master looked at her. 'Yes, he is most strange, isn't he? I expect you've never seen anything like this on Earth.'

Paul dug her sharply in the ribs. 'Er – no,' she said.

'Now, talking of Earth, I've always felt that what this museum needs is a good exhibit from that planet. And whatever could be better than two real Earth children and their flying machine?'

And, grinning, he snapped his fingers. Straight away, the two purple men pushed the children into the cage beside Prunes, and the bicycle into the cage next to them, and slammed the doors.

'I hope you are happy in your

new home, my dears,' said the master, grinning again. 'Tomorrow, experiments will begin on the flying machine to find out how it works. Goodbye.'

'Crumbs,' said Prunes after he'd gone. 'Fancy meeting you two.'

'Oh Prunes, it's lovely to see you,' said Sue. 'But what are you doing here?'

Prunes explained that he was on the edge of the land of the Horribles exploring, when a purple space craft captured him and took him to Purple Three. 'Mind you, I wasn't very sorry,' he continued. 'I had to share a very damp hole with a slug family. Though this place isn't much better,' he said, looking sadly through the bars.

‘However are we going to get out?’ said Paul. ‘Even if we get out of the cages, there’s still that guard to get past.’

Sue began to cry. She didn’t want to be locked up in a purple cage for the rest of her life. ‘The only thing that can help us is the bicycle,’ she said. ‘Bicycle, please help us to get out of here.’

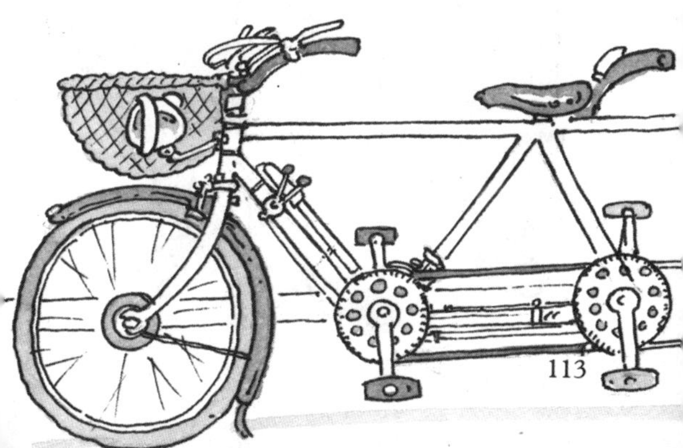

But the bicycle just leant against the cage bars.

And then a mysterious voice said, ‘Paul, look in your pocket.’

So Paul did and, to his amazement, he found a pair of bicycle clips.

‘Now call the guard over and, when he’s close, throw the bicycle clips at him.’

Paul looked at Sue and Prunes. Who was saying these words? ‘Oh well, we’ve got nothing to lose,’ he said.

So Sue shouted out to the guard that she wasn’t feeling very well. The guard came over and, when he was close, Paul threw the bicycle clips at him. As they

travelled through the air they turned into handcuffs – and snapped the guard's wrists to the bars of the cage!

Quickly, Sue reached for the keys on the guard's belt and unlocked the cages.

'Serves you right, you silly little purple man,' said Prunes rudely, sticking out his tongue.

The guard was so angry that his

face grew more and more purple. Suddenly they noticed his middle eye was flashing and a squeaking sound was coming from it.

'That's the alarm bell. Time to get out of here,' said Prunes, leaping into the bicycle basket. 'This is just like old times.'

Quickly, the children pushed the bicycle through the museum. They were almost free! But then, when they got outside, they found they were surrounded by little purple men holding purple machine guns.

'Crumbs, we've had it now,' said Prunes. And then suddenly the bicycle's front light shone a strange bright yellow light into the purple men's faces. They started

squeaking and backing away in terror.

The children leapt on to the bicycle and off they flew, leaving behind them hundreds of squeaking, frightened little purple men.

'Phew, that was a close one,' said Prunes. 'The bicycle certainly saved the day there.'

'Yes, three cheers for the bicycle,' said Sue. 'Hip hip . . .'

'HURRAY!' they shouted.

'I'd still like to know how those bicycle clips came to be in my pocket,' said Paul.

'By magic, of course,' said Sue. 'Surely you must believe in it *now*!'

# The land of the giants

Performing all those magical tricks on Purple Three left the bicycle rather tired, and it flew lower than it normally did. Twice it almost hit a tree or a bird and then it really did hit something, and so they had to stop. The thing that they'd hit was rather like a smooth brown hill.

'Where are we?' asked Sue.

'You're not going to believe this,' said Prunes. 'But I think we're stuck in the rim of a giant's hat.'

'Very funny,' said Paul.

And then both they and the hill were moving downwards until they were right next to the biggest face they'd ever seen. The wrinkles in the giant's forehead were like red railway lines, his eyebrows were like two ginger forests, his eyes were as big as dart boards, his nostrils were like caves and his mouth – well, it was big

enough to eat them all up in one gulp.

'Well, well, well, what has landed in the brim of my hat?' boomed the giant and laughed so loudly that the children and Prunes were not only deafened, but were almost blown away. It felt just like a hurricane – a rather oniony hurricane, for the giant

had eaten no less than ten jars of pickled onions for his lunch. The onions made them all cry.

'Oh no, don't cry,' bellowed the giant. 'I'm not going to hurt you. I'm going to take you back to my house and give you a good meal. I expect you'd prefer to walk than have me carry you,' and he lowered them gently to the ground.

'I don't trust this giant bloke. I

think we should get out of here while the going's good,' whispered Prunes. But the bicycle was too tired to fly. 'Oh well, we're stuck here now,' he said. 'Crumbs, I don't half feel small.'

They all did. Their heads just came up to the giant's pink boot laces, and what hard work it was walking. To the giant it just

seemed like an ordinary road, but to them every stone was like a mountain, every hole a great deep valley.

'Now I know what an ant must feel like,' puffed Prunes.

Suddenly, in front of them, they saw the biggest house they'd ever seen. If they put their heads right back they could just see the roof.

At the door stood the giant's wife, who was as huge as he was.

'What have you got there, Rumble?' she asked. (Rumble was the giant's name.) 'Oh my, two dear little children, a bicycle, and er . . .'

'Prunes is the name,' shouted Prunes.

'Ah, now let me take a closer look at you all,' she said and picked them up in her huge, pink, squashy hand. 'You poor little things, you're as light as feathers. You must be starving,' she said, and took them into the kitchen, where two whole oxen were roasting on a spit. A cook in a hat as high as a chimney pot and with

arms as thick as oak trees was preparing an apple pie that was the size of a lorry. Prunes' eyes almost popped out of his head. He'd never seen so much food in his life.

'Meet our new guests,' said the giant's wife to the cook. 'This is er . . .'

'Paul, Sue, and I'm Prunes,' said Prunes.

'And my name's Bumble and this is Cook,' said Bumble.

'I hope you've got good appetites,' said Cook, grinning. Her teeth were the size of saucers, and looked rather sharp.

'You bet,' said Prunes.

At supper, while the bicycle rested under a huge daisy in the garden, Paul, Sue and Prunes ate between them one roast chicken, two legs of pork, three hamburgers, four roast potatoes, five large pieces of apple pie, six scoops of ice cream, and a giant strawberry milk shake each to wash it all down. But if you think that's a lot, you should have seen how much

Rumble and Bumble ate! A whole ox each, forty-two potatoes (Prunes counted), a mountain of runner beans, the rest of the apple pie (which, remember, was the size of a lorry), and enough ice cream to fill two bath tubs.

'Wow!' said Prunes, patting his very round tummy. 'For the first time in ages I feel almost full.'

When they had finally finished

eating, the children told the giants all their adventures. The giants laughed at the funny bits and cried at the sad bits.

'My dears,' said Bumble when they had finished, 'you must be exhausted after all those adventures. Rumble and I insist that you make our house your home. We would be delighted to have you, and you can stay for as long as you like.'

Later, when the three of them were tucked up in a bed as big as a swimming pool, Prunes said, 'You know, I wouldn't mind living here. All the food you can eat, a comfortable bed, a roof over your head. I think I'll take Bumble up

on her offer.' Then, after such an enormous supper, he fell fast asleep.

The next few days passed very pleasantly. They ate more food than they'd ever eaten in their lives. 'It's almost as if they're trying to fatten us up,' said Sue. They

played some great games of hide-and-seek, for there were so many places to hide! Once Prunes hid in the bowl of Rumble's pipe, and they didn't find him for hours. And often, after supper, the giants would allow them to climb over them. What fun it was trying to climb up Rumble's waistcoat buttons, or swinging on Bumble's bonnet ribbons! Meanwhile, the bicycle had its very own home in an empty rabbit hutch, and the children visited it every day to make sure it was all right.

One day it started to rain, so they stayed in their room. They were busy turning one of Rumble's old boots into a house, when suddenly there was a tap-tap on the window. It was the bicycle!

'I wonder what it wants,' said Paul.

'It must be urgent,' said Sue. 'Come on.'

So, after managing to open the great big window, they climbed on. Then the bicycle flew to the kitchen window, and hovered beside it.

Inside, they could see that Bumble and Cook were arguing. Horrified, they listened to what they were saying.

'Children are far better baked than roasted. Everyone knows that.'

'But my recipe book says, "Sprinkle a few herbs over and

roast until crisp." And this book has never been wrong yet.'

'Oh, have it your own way then,' said Bumble. 'And what about that Prunes creature?'

Cook shook her head. 'Shall I cook him the way I would a mouse?'

And then they spotted the bicycle. Their normally jolly faces turned white with rage. 'They're escaping! After fattening them up, they're escaping,' shouted

Bumble, and hurled the rolling pin at them. It came crashing through the window but the bicycle nimbly managed to dodge it, and flew up into the sky. Below them they could hear the thundering feet and deafening roars of three very angry giants.

'Come back!' they bellowed.

'No fear,' shouted Prunes.

'Well,' said Sue when they were safely out of the giants' reach. 'To think they were going to eat us! You can't trust anyone.'

'And they seemed so nice and kind,' said Paul. 'If it hadn't been for the bicycle we'd be sizzling in that oven.'

'Yes, thanks old pal,' said Prunes, slapping the handle bars. 'Mouse indeed. Hmph! Well, I won't be making that place my home after all.'

'Never mind,' said Sue. 'Perhaps you'll like the next place.'

'Bet the food won't be so good,' said Prunes, slapping his now extremely round tummy. 'Crumbs, I could do with a strawberry milk shake and a hamburger or two right now!'

# Knickerbocker Glory

'Crumbs,' said Prunes after they'd only been flying for a minute. 'What's got into the bicycle?' For it had started to dance and prance about in the sky like a circus horse.

And then it was landing in green

hilly countryside, right next to a policeman. Not an ordinary policeman, mind you, for there were two very odd things about him. One was that although he had a policeman's helmet, he was wearing pyjamas. The other was, he was directing traffic. And the odd thing about that was, there was no traffic in sight.

'Excuse me, could you tell us the name of this place?' asked Sue.

The policeman continued to direct traffic while speaking. 'That depends on what day of the week it is,' he said. 'On Sunday it's called Knickerbocker Glory, on Monday it's called Back to School, on Tuesday it's called

Hang out the Washing, on Wednesday it's called Ugh, the Middle of the Week, on Thursday it's called Anything You Like, on Friday it's called Hurray, It's Friday, on . . .' And then he suddenly stopped talking and blew on a tin whistle. 'Can't park there,' he said, pointing at the bicycle.

'Where can we park then?' asked Sue, trying not to laugh.

'Turn left at the greengrocer's, first right after the butcher's, down to the end next to the toy-shop. You'll find a nice elephant park there.'

The children looked round. All they could see were hills and trees.

And had he said *elephant park*? 'This is a bicycle, not an elephant,' said Paul.

'Bicycles – elephants – they're all much of a muchness,' said the policeman. 'Now please remove it straight away, it's causing a traffic jam.'

Trying hard not to giggle, they

wheeled the bicycle over to a large tree and leant it up against the trunk. It didn't look much like an elephant park, but the policeman seemed happy enough.

Suddenly they realized that Prunes wasn't with them. They were just about to go and look for him, when a voice above them said, 'What's purple, lives in a watering can and snores?'

They looked up and saw an owl peering down at them from a hole in the tree. He wore a crimson bow tie and seemed to be winking at them.

'Give up,' said Sue.

'A kangaroo going to school, of course. I thought everyone knew that.'

'But that doesn't make sense,' said Paul. 'A kangaroo isn't . . .'

'Everything makes sense if you want it to,' said the owl crossly. 'I'll ask you another. What's green and eats its breakfast standing up?'

'A one-legged cabbage,' Paul whispered to Sue as a joke.

'Did I hear you say a one-legged cabbage? Well, that's just too bad,' said the owl, upset now. 'You must have heard it before. You're nothing but a cheat.'

'We'd better go,' said Paul. 'Prunes could be in trouble.'

'Oh, don't go,' said the owl. 'I want to ask you some more jokes. I know four-hundred-and-thirty-seven altogether, and you've only heard two. That leaves – er . . .'

'Four-hundred-and-thirty-five,' said Sue. 'But I'm afraid we've got to find our friend Prunes.'

'Ah-ha,' said the owl. 'I know an excellent joke about prunes. What goes clank-clank-bonk, clank-clank-bonk, every third

Sunday of the month?'

'Prunes,' Sue and Paul said together.

'Wrong!' roared the owl, almost falling out of his hole with glee. 'A ferret in a bowler hat. Hee, hee, fooled you!'

The children excused themselves and ran off before bursting out laughing. Everyone in this place was as nutty as a fruitcake. They had only just finished laughing when they saw a man with a fried egg on his head and that almost started them off again.

'Excuse me, have you seen a tubby, furry green animal by the name of Prunes?' Sue asked him, trying hard not to laugh.

The man, missing the fried egg, scratched his head.

'Now, let's think. Well, I'll tell you what animals I *have* seen today,' he said and grinned, revealing blue, green, mauve and pink teeth. 'I've seen Mrs Tortoise in a new hat; I've seen Billy Goat having his beard trimmed; I've seen that hedgehog fellow trying to tap-dance; and while I was at the dentist having my teeth painted, I saw Lizzie Lizard.'

'But I didn't think lizards had any teeth,' said Paul.

The man with the fried egg on his head looked surprised. 'They don't. But why should that stop them going to the dentist?

Now, where was I? Oh yes, and I saw Stoat washing his new go-cart. And that's all. So the short answer is, no I haven't seen a tubby, furry green animal by the name of Prunes. Good morning!'

The children started climbing a hill. On the way they met a man wearing a flower-pot hat, a tie made out of a piece of garden hose and carrying a watering can which he was using as a shopping basket.

'Excuse me, have you seen a tubby, furry green animal by the name of Prunes?' they asked.

The man looked in his watering can. 'Not today, I'm afraid,' he

said. 'Come back next Thursday, and I might have one then.'

So they walked a bit further up the hill and saw a horse sunbathing in a deckchair. He wore bathing trunks and sunglasses.

'Excuse me, have you seen a tubby, furry green animal by the name of Prunes?' they asked.

'That,' said the horse, 'depends on what you mean by green. You see, because I'm wearing sunglasses, all animals look black to me. I did see a tubby, furry black animal walk up the hill. He could have been green for all I know.'

So Paul and Sue walked to the top of the hill. There they met a pig wearing a cap and on roller skates.

'Excuse me, have you seen a tubby, furry green animal by the

name of Prunes?' they asked.

The pig raised his trotter to his mouth and giggled. 'He's over under that tree,' he said. 'But he isn't alone.'

And there he was, holding the paw of a tubby, furry animal just like Prunes, except that instead of being bright green it was bright yellow.

Prunes waved and went over to them. 'Hello, old pals,' he said. He looked rather embarrassed.

‘Look, I know that love and all that is soppy old stuff,’ he said. ‘But . . . well, it’s happened. I’ve fallen in love with the most beautiful girl in the world – er, the universe – oh, wherever we are.’

Paul and Sue looked over at the yellow animal. She didn’t look very beautiful to them, but then they weren’t Prunes.

'And guess what her name is,' said Prunes. 'Custard! Prunes and Custard! You see, we were made for each other.'

Paul and Sue laughed, and Sue threw her arms round his furry neck. 'I am pleased,' she said. 'You've found somewhere where you'll be happy at last.'

They went over and said hello to Custard, and you know what she said? Yes, she said, 'Crumbs!'

'You two really are made for each other,' said Sue, laughing. 'Well, we'd better be going. We're already days late for tea!'

The policeman in pyjamas, the man with the fried egg on his head, the man with the watering-can

shopping basket, the owl in the crimson bow tie, the horse in bathing trunks and the pig on roller skates, not to mention Prunes and Custard, all came to wave goodbye.

The policeman blew his whistle. ‘You’re going too fast. Please accompany me to the police station,’ he shouted as they took off into the sky, but the children just laughed and waved.

‘What wears blue socks and watches television with its eyes closed?’ panted the owl, flying along beside them.

‘Prunes,’ said Paul.

‘Custard,’ giggled Sue.

‘Wrong,’ said the owl triumphantly. ‘A lesser-spotted woodpecker. *Everyone* knows that!’

# The land of magic

---

'If Prunes was still with us he would say "Crumbs",' joked Paul as they looked round at this magical place. Twisted old witches' cottages peered over the brows of hills, and smoke rose up from the chimneys of elves' and goblins' homes in the roots of trees. In the distance, turreted castles clung to the crags of rocky mountains.

Suddenly, a wizard in a blue sparkling suit and a shiny top hat appeared at their sides. 'I say, that's ever such an unusual bicycle you've got there, isn't it,' he said. 'I can sense its magical powers from here.' He ran his long thin fingers, that were covered in glittering rings as big as strawberries, all over it. 'Tell you what,' he said. 'I'll give you all my jewels – ever so valuable, they are – in return for this bicycle.'

'I'm sorry, but we'd never part

with it,' said Sue, holding firmly on to the handlebars. 'But surely you must have magical powers yourself. Why can't you just magic yourself one?'

The wizard burst into tears. 'This is terrifically embarrassing,' he said, blowing his nose on a silver handkerchief. 'I trust you can keep a secret? You see, here's me living in a land of magic, and I've quite forgotten how to perform magical tricks. At first I pretended I could still do them – you

know, placing a frog under my hat which I said had got there by magic, and so on. But people have begun to suspect I'm just a cheat – a fraud. And the worst thing of all is, if they can prove I no longer have magical powers, they will turn me out of my castle and I will be homeless.'

The children felt very sorry for the wizard, and wished there was some way they could help him. Suddenly, a very strange thing happened. The bicycle pump flew through the air and landed in the wizard's hand. The wizard's eyes nearly popped out of his head. 'I say,' he said. 'Do you think it could be a *magical* bicycle pump?'

'Give it a try,' said Paul.

So the wizard cleared his throat and said, 'Bicycle pump, I want you to turn that dandelion into a chocolate ice cream.'

And, before their very eyes, the dandelion did turn into an ice cream!

'You can keep the pump if you like,' said Sue.

The wizard's tears turned to tears of joy. 'How can I ever thank you enough, my dears,' he said, hugging both the children and the bicycle.

Meanwhile, a crowd of witches, goblins, fairies and magicians had surrounded them.

'That stupid wizard has no more magical powers than a mouldy potato,' said a witch.

'He's a complete fraud,' said a goblin.

'Oh yes?' said the wizard. 'Well allow me to prove you wrong,' and, with a swish of the bicycle pump, turned the witch's hat into a banana and the goblin's shoes into carrots.

Their mouths dropped open in amazement. So he wasn't a fraud,

after all. The wizard beamed round at them. This was the moment he'd been dreaming about for months – no, years!

And then Sue asked him if he could magic them home, they were now *weeks* late for tea.

'It's the very least I can do, my dears,' said the happy wizard. 'And now, ladies and gentlemen,' he announced, 'I'm going to magic these two children and the bicycle through the air and back to Earth.' After giving a bow, he waved the pump, and suddenly

they were whizzing as fast as an aeroplane over all the places they'd visited.

'This is like seeing a speeded-up film backwards,' laughed Sue as they passed over Prunes and Custard still holding hands on the hill; over the giants' house where Rumble, Bumble and Cook were still roaring and shaking their fists; over the silent world of the

three-eyed purple men and the bone-shaped Planet of the Dogs. They passed over the Land of the Horribles, and then the palace where the king still had a bald head and the queen still had green teeth. They passed over the mad witch flying on her cat and then, before they knew it, with a thud and a skid, they were back in the

bushes at the end of their garden, where all their adventures had begun. The bicycle disappeared from beneath them and Father was still calling tea-time. And there was William, bouncing across the lawn!

'Oh, Father,' they panted, running up to him. 'We're so sorry we're late. You see . . .'

'Late?' said their father, looking surprised. 'But I've only called tea-time twice. Usually I have to call far more times before you come.'

The children were astonished. 'But we've been away for days and days,' Sue said. 'We thought you'd have the police out looking for us.'

They all went into the kitchen to join Mother and, while William wolfed down a bowl of dog biscuits, they began to tell them all about their adventures.

They had just got to the bit

where Prunes was pulling faces at the Horribles, when their parents burst out laughing.

'Really, what imaginations you children have,' said Father.

Paul and Sue looked at them, furious. 'You don't believe us, do you?' said Paul. 'You think we're making it all up.'

Mother wiped her eyes on the tea towel. 'Darlings, how could all